# Lenten Worship For Young Adults

## Ellery Lane

CSS Publishing Company, Inc., Lima, Ohio

LENTEN WORSHIP FOR YOUNG ADULTS

Revised edition © 1997

Copyright © 1972 by
CSS Publishing Company, Inc.
Lima, Ohio

The original purchaser may photocopy material in this publication for use as it was intended (i.e. worship material for worship use; educational material for classroom use; dramatic material for staging or production). No additional permission is required from the publisher for such copying by the original purchaser only. Inquiries should be addressed to: Permissions, CSS Publishing Company, Inc., P.O. Box 4503, Lima, Ohio 45802-4503.

ISBN: 0-7880-1015-8                                   PRINTED IN U.S.A.

## Preface

The services in this volume are intended for use in an evening series for Lent. There is a variety of presentations: the first service involves seven lay leaders from the congregation in addition to the pastor or lay leader. The third service involves the entire congregation, reading parts of the lessons and liturgy alternately as the congregation is divided into sections. The other four services are set up as dialogues, involving four to six young people and the pastor.

Hymns are suggestions; others may be substituted, if desired, in keeping with the theme of each presentation.

The meditations, in the form of discussions, can be presented in about 15 minutes each. There are no required props or special worship settings; in one of the dialogues a few signs are suggested.

## Table Of Contents

| | |
|---|---|
| A Service Based On The Seven Last Words | 7 |
| A Call To Service | 15 |
| An Evening Service For Lent | 21 |
| A Service Based On Theological Concepts | 27 |
| A Service Based On The Sacrament Of Baptism | 39 |
| A Service Based On The Sacrament Of The Altar | 47 |

## A Service Based On The Seven Last Words

(For the meditation on the seven words, different members of the congregation may be given sections to read. They may remain in their places rather than coming to the altar.)

**Pastor:** O Lord, open my lips.

**Cong.:** **And my mouth shall speak your praise.**

**Pastor:** Be pleased, O God, to deliver me.

**Cong.:** **O Lord, make haste to help me.**

**All:** **Glory be to the Father and to the Son and to the Holy Spirit; as it was in the beginning, is now, and shall be forever and ever. Amen. Praise be to you.**

**The Psalm:** Psalm 22

**The Gloria Patri** (may be said or sung)

**The Lesson**

**The Hymn:** "O Perfect Life Of Love"

**The Kyrie** (may be said or sung)

**The Prayer:**
   Our Father in heaven:
    Holy be your name,
    Your kingdom come,
    Your will be done
     on earth as in heaven.
    Give us today our daily bread.

Forgive us our sins
    as we forgive those who sin against us.
Save us in the time of trial,
    and deliver us from evil.
For yours is the kingdom, the power,
    and the glory forever. Amen.

**Meditation Hymn:** "Wide Open Are Thy Hands"

**Meditation Responsive Readings** On The Seven Last Words

I.     "Father, forgive them; for they know not what they do"

    Father, forgive us our thoughtlessness

        toward the old and forgotten — help us to remember that one day we too shall be old and helpless; teach us your patience when they are slow to understand and accept change; help us to recognize that they are aching to be free from the burdens of age and infirmity; let us show compassion as you have shown compassion to us.

        toward the lost and friendless — make us see our own selfishness and complacency; make us remember that each one, no matter how low he or she has fallen, is still your creature and our brother or sister; remind us that Jesus was not too proud to go among the outcasts of society.

        toward the guilty and alienated — reminded us that we too are liable to fall into sin and despair at any moment; remind us that it is your grace, not our own efforts, that are our salvation; give us the gift of forgiveness, as you have forgiven us.

toward those who are different from us — let us recognize that the outward layer of a person is nothing; it is the inner person that matters and in God's sight all men are the same; help us to be tolerant of differences in custom and understanding — let us grow in knowledge and wisdom as we learn to accept others for what they are, not what we would like them be.

II. "Today shalt thou be with me in Paradise"

Lord,

Help us in sickness — to look toward you with trust that you will guide the physician's hands and skills to cure our ills.

help us when we are in danger of dying — that we learn to accept death as a friend which releases us from pain in this life to a life of joy and everlasting peace with you.

help us when are afraid — to see you near us and to feel your presence comforting and sustaining us in all times of fear and agony.

help us at every moment to put our lives in your hands with complete confidence, knowing that, whatever happens, you have promised to take us to yourself.

III. "Woman, behold thy son!" "Behold thy mother!"

Father,

As we look to you as our great and loving Father, help us

to love and respect our earthly parents at all times, always recognizing that they are human and so liable to make mistakes.

to know that even in times of great personal trouble, our parents will follow your example and do what is best for us, rather than for themselves.

as parents, to know that the gift of children is a sign of your love and that we are to cherish and love our children and to raise them to know and love you as we do.

IV. "My God, my God, why hast thou forsaken me?"

Merciful God,

Be with us when

we are hurt and frightened and we cannot find you near. Don't let us despair, but let us know that you are watching over us.

the world and its problems threaten to overwhelm us; let us know that you are above the pettiness of men and that we need only turn to you for our solutions.

the world and its pleasures threaten to alienate us from you; teach us that all lasting pleasure comes from service to you and eternal joy comes only from your boundless love.

we feel lost and deserted and alone; speak to us in your loving voice and let us know that we are protected under the shadow of your hand, and that nothing can harm us.

V. "I thirst."

Dearest Jesus,

Help us to show compassion for those who are with out; let us give food and drink to the needy, as you have done for us.

Help us when we thirst for knowledge of you and your love; show us the way to eternal salvation through yourself.

Help us to spread the knowledge of your loving concern to all those others who are thirsting for hope and help; teach us how to teach them.

VI.     "It is finished"

Gracious Father,

Teach us

that each person has an allotted time on earth and that each one has an obligation to help one's fellow human beings during that time.

that none of us can accomplish all things, but that you only demand that we do the best of which we are capable; it is folly to attempt what we know we cannot achieve.

that it is not shameful to know and accept our limitations; it is only shameful to refuse to do what we can.

that for everything there is an end — for humans, beasts, and seasons; when that end has arrived for us, help us to say with dignity, "It is finished."

VII.     "Father, into thy hands I commend my spirit"

Loving God,

When the hour of death approaches,

help us to come to you with joy and gladness, knowing that we will no longer suffer or be afraid.

help our loved ones to know that we are not afraid, but that we lean on your loving breast and are at peace.

help us to die with dignity, so that even our dying, as well as our living, will be a witness to you.

**The Creed** (The pastor shall say: And now let us confess our faith in the words of the Apostles' Creed.)

I believe in God the Father, the Almighty,
   creator of heaven and earth.
I believe in Jesus Christ, his only Son, our Lord,
   who was conceived by the power of the Holy
   Spirit and born of the Virgin Mary.
   He suffered and was crucified under Pontius Pilate.
   He died and was buried.
   He went to the dead,
   and on the third day he rose again.
   He entered into heaven
   and is seated at the right hand of God the
   Almighty Father.
   He will come again to judge the living and the dead.
I believe in the Holy spirit,
   the holy catholic Church,
   the communion of saints,
   the forgiveness of sins,
   the resurrection of the body,
   and the life eternal. Amen.

**The Offering**

**The Prayer:**

**Pastor:** We thank you, heavenly Father, through Jesus Christ, your dear Son, that you have kept us this day;

and we pray that you will forgive us all our sins where we have done wrong, and keep us this night also.

For into your hands we commend ourselves, our bodies and souls, and all things. Let your holy angel be with us that the wicked Foe may have no power over us. Amen.

**The Benediction**

## A Call To Service

**Pastor:** O Lord, open my lips.

**Cong.:** **And my mouth shall speak your praise.**

**Pastor:** Be pleased, O God, to deliver me.

**Cong.:** **O Lord, make haste to help me.**

**All:** **Glory be to the Father and to the Son and to the Holy Spirit; as it was in the beginning, is now, and shall be forever and ever. Amen. Praise be to you.**

**The Psalm:** Psalm 25

**The Gloria Patri** (may be said or sung)

**The Lesson**

Leader: All of us, at one time or another, have said, "I'd really like to help somebody else, I'd like to show my faith and my love in service, but I don't know how." Well, tonight we want to conduct our service around the idea of showing God's love through our lives. First of all, let's set the mood by singing the hymn "O Brother Man."

**Hymn:** "O Brother Man"

(During the singing of the hymn, the actors may take seats on the steps or in the nave. There should be four young people and the pastor.)

1st Boy: You know the other day I was on the bus, and I heard a man in front of me say to the man with him, "Boy, here they come again with all the appeals for money.

What do they think we're made of? Gold? I'm no slacker. I give to the United Way, and I even give to some other charities. And every now and then I put something into the benevolence fund at church. What more do they want? Blood? Yeah, come to think of it, I've been asked to give that, too! Where does it all end? I work hard for my money, so let those lazy bums that expect charity go out and earn their way. I do all I can, and that's that!" You all know how I like dramatics, and that made me think — a picture just sort of-formed itself in front of my eyes. What do you think of this as an opening scene:

We open on a hill somewhere in Galilee. Seated on the mountain is a man in a simple white robe. And seated at his feet are a lot of people, listening intently to what he has to say. Soft music plays in the background, as the man says in a strangely thrilling voice:

"Blessed are the poor in spirit, for theirs is the kingdom of heaven. Blessed are those who mourn, for they shall be comforted. Blessed are the meek, for they shall inherit the earth." The music swells, there is an unearthly light playing about the face of the man on the hill. And then slowly the music and the light fade away. Cut. End of scene. And then another segment, with just the sound of the man's voice saying, "Father, forgive them." What do you think?

1st Girl: Yes, I see what it is you're driving at, _____. I guess it's the same thing that makes me want to go into social work when I finish school. There are so many people around who need help of one kind or another, and I want to give them that help. I think that's what Jesus wants me to do. His time was spent with the unfortunates of the world — not sitting around at home waiting for them to come to him, but going out to where they were. I suppose that if he'd wanted to, he could have made a good thing out of his powers. He could have rented a store front close to the Temple and hung his shingle out in front. And, for a fee, the authorities would have looked the other way. But that wouldn't have helped the penniless and the destitute and the forsaken. No, all he would have accomplished that way would have been to shut himself off from those who needed his help. Instead, he says, "You to whom the problems of the world are overwhelming, you who are tired of fighting the battles of life, come, and find my rest." But they don't always know how to find that way. And so I want to give my life to helping them find it.

Pastor: I'm very glad to hear you say that, _____. You know, we hear so often on our radios that "poverty hurts." That's true — but there's a poverty of the spirit that also hurts. Each time I fail to help my brother or sister who is in need, I become poorer in spirit. Each time I turn my back on a cry for help, my personal stock goes lower. But each time I respond in love to another's need, I am witnessing for Christ. How do you think we relate this idea to this time of Lent?

2nd Boy: Well, I think that's easy enough. Jesus died for us on Good Friday and he suffered a lot before he was allowed to die, but he was willing to do it because he loved us so much. And he wants us to love our fellow human beings enough to give up some things for them and maybe suffer a little for them, too. The whole thing is based on love. Sort of like saying, "I love you" in actions, not in words. Sometimes people think you can only witness through talking about God or through reading the Bible and being a regular churchgoer and that sort of thing. Well, of course, that's necessary, too, but I have to show my love or just talking doesn't mean a thing.

2nd Girl: That's right. I was just sitting here thinking about the parable of the Good Samaritan. I don't know of any place in the parable where he sat down and preached to the man who was beaten by robbers. He didn't say, "Brother, I'm going to tell you about the love of God, and then we'll go along to an inn and I'll fix you up." No, he loved all right, but that love showed itself in action. His love was mixed with the oil and the wine that he poured on the man's wounds, and that love healed the man's spirit, as the ointments healed his body. And I can think of so many other ways in which we could show that same love. You know, things like going out to visit the old and the helpless. I've been out to some old folks' homes, and they're so often so unhappy, just because no one cares enough to come to see them.

1st Boy: Yeah, or how about the children in the hospitals for the retarded or the physically handicapped? They're human, too, even though sometimes they don't seem to be more than living vegetables. But they're still our responsibility.

2nd Boy: Yes, and how about the people in town whose racial or ethnic heritage is different from ours? You know, once I heard someone say, "Oh, they don't really want to worship with us. They have churches of their own, and they're happier with their own kind." But I don't know what they mean by that. Seems to me that they're God's children, and that's a good kind to be. So what if their skin's a different color from mine! Or maybe they're not quite as well dressed! That's all on the outside, and the outside layer isn't very important anyway. Whenever I think about that, I think of all the people who say, "What do you expect us to do? After all, we're good churchgoing Christians, we fulfill our pledges, we serve on a committee now and then. What more do you want from us? You're certainly not asking us to throw over all our favorite prejudices!" Well, maybe they can work that out with their own consciences, but for me, I don't want to be one of those to whom the Lord will say, "Sorry, but there was that time when you looked down your noses at one of my children. So I think maybe you'd better just step aside here and let some of my real followers take the front seats."

1st Girl: You know, I think that everything that we've been saying here tonight is the whole emphasis of Lent. Jesus willingly gave up his life on the cross for the old people and the handicapped and the children and the alienated, as well as for those of us who hide behind our comfortable lives and refuse to commit ourselves. Well, I for one intend to let the message of Lent be my personal commitment to serving Jesus through serving my fellow man.

Pastor: Yes, I think you have really understood the Lenten message. Just a few days before his final agony, Jesus said to his disciples, "Then the king will say to those on his right: 'Come, you have won my Father's blessing.' Take your inheritance — the kingdom reserved for you since the foundation of the world! For I was hungry and you gave me food. I was thirsty and you gave me a drink. I was lonely and you made me welcome. I was naked and you clothed me. I was ill and you came and looked after me. I was in prison and you came to see me there."

Then the true men will answer him: "Lord, when did we see you hungry and give you food? When did we see you thirsty and give you something to drink? When did we see you lonely and make you welcome, or see you naked and clothe you, or see you ill or in prison and go to see you?"

And the king will reply, "I assure you that whatever you did for the humblest of my brothers you did for me." As Jesus gave his life for others, so we too are called to give our lives in service to others. God has given each of us certain talents, and he expects that we use these talents to serve him. And I think you have all recognized this fact. Let's emphasize this even more by singing the hymn "O Master, Let Me Walk With Thee."

**Hymn:** "O Master, Let Me Walk With Thee"

Pastor: Let us conclude our service by asking God's help for our endeavors and his blessing as we strive to serve our fellow man:

Our Father, as we face the days and years ahead of us, help us to remember that the love which you showed for us in permitting your own beloved Son to suffer the agonies of the cross so that we might be saved, also demands that we respond in love in return. When we become discouraged in our dealings with others, sustain us with your love; when we are heartsick over a lost soul, comfort us with your love; when we are mocked and scorned because of our concern, strengthen us with your love; and when we are tired of the burden of the world's indifference, uphold us with your love. For your love is all that we need. We ask it in the name of our suffering Savior, your Son, Jesus Christ our Lord.

## An Evening Service For Lent

**Pastor:** O Lord, open my lips.

**Cong.:** **And my mouth shall speak your praise.**

**Pastor:** Be pleased, O God, to deliver me.

**Cong.:** **O Lord, make haste to help me.**

**All:** **Glory be to the Father and to the Son and to the Holy Spirit; as it was in the beginning, is now, and shall be forever and ever. Amen. Praise be to you.**

**The Psalm:** Paraphrase of Psalm 1

**Pastor:** The man who chooses to live a significant life is not going to take his cues from the religiously indifferent.

**Cong.:** **Nor will he conform to the crowd
Nor mouth his prejudices
Nor dote on the failures of others.**

**Pastor:** His ultimate concern is the will of God.

**Cong.:** **He makes his daily decisions in respect to that will.**

**Pastor:** He can be compared to a sturdy tree planted in rich and moist soil.

**Cong.:** **As the tree yields fruit, so his life manifests blessing for others, his life is productive and effective.**

**Pastor:** This is not true concerning the ungodly.

**Cong.:** **They are like sand in a desert storm. Or leaves in an autumn wind.**

**Pastor:** They cannot stand against the judgments of the eternal God.

**Cong.:** **And they are most uncomfortable amongst those who demonstrate genuine faith in the God of righteousness.**

**Pastor:** The children of God walk in the course that God has ordained.

**Cong.:** **The children of unbelief walk in paths of self-destruction.**

**The Gloria Patri** (may be said or sung)

**The Lesson**

**Hymn:** "They'll Know We Are Christians By Our Love"

**Meditation** (Responsive Reading of a Parable)

Leader: That which was from the beginning, which we have heard, which we have seen with our eyes, which we have looked upon, our hands have handled, of the Word of life ... declare we ... (1 John 1-2).

Reader: (Luke 10-37) And behold, a certain lawyer stood up, and tempted him saying, "Master, what shall I do to inherit eternal life?" He said unto him, "What is written in the Law? How readest thou?" And he answering said, "Thou shalt love the Lord thy God with all thy heart and with all thy soul, and with all thy strength, and with all thy mind; and thy neighbor as thyself." And he said unto him, "Thou hast answered right. This do and thou shalt live." But he, willing to justify himself, said unto Jesus, "And who is my neighbor?"

And Jesus answering said, "A certain man went down from Jerusalem to Jericho, and fell among thieves."

(The Congregation responds as indicated: right side as Congregation 1, left side as Congregation 2.)

**Congregation 1:** Lord of thieves, as well as the rest of humankind, change their warped lives. But keep us all from committing thievery unawares ...

**Congregation 2:** Lord, whose household is the world and more, let us not be party to unjust housing practices. Bring justice to our land for those who are in slums because they cannot be elsewhere.

Reader: Who stripped him of his raiment and wounded him, and departed, leaving him half-dead.

**Congregation 1:** O Christ, friend of the friendless, the world is filled with victims; let us begin to minister with resolution to those in our own block. Restore those who lack moral resolution; strengthen the weak; comfort the dying.

**Congregation 2:** And give us humanity enough to know that thieves may also fall among thieves. Forgive us our negligence of prisoners and prisons ...

**Congregation 1:** And save us from a pride that thinks that we may never fall among the thieves ...

Reader: And by chance there came down a certain priest that way; and when he saw him, he passed by on the other side.

**Congregation 1:** Lord, keep us from "the other side" where blindness is.

Reader: And likewise a Levite, when he was at the place, came and looked on him, and passed by on the other side.

**Congregation 2:** O Christ, who gave us the name of Christian, let us not use our name or thine in vain.

Reader: But a certain Samaritan, as he journeyed, came where he was and when he saw him, he had compassion on him.

**Congregation 1:** Lord of the gospel, teach us that no man knows the gospel who does not know compassion.

**Congregation 2:** O Spirit of the Living God, breathe into us the love that bears all things, believes all things, hopes all things, endures all things, the love that never fails.

Reader: And the Samaritan went to him, and bound up his wounds, pouring in oil and wine, and set him on his own beast, and brought him to an inn, and took care of him.

**Congregation 1:** O Christ, who did not come to be ministered unto, but to minister, fulfill in us thy ministry.

**Congregation 2:** We pray for those who daily carry on this ministry in special areas of the life of the church in the world. Keep them from tiredness or despair. Give them rich resources of the gospel, the wells of thy love.

Reader: And on the morrow when he departed, he took out two pence, and gave them to the host, and said unto him, "Take care of him; and whatsoever thou spendest more, when I come again I will repay thee."

**Congregation 1:** Help us to receive every moment of life and every person in life as gifts from God. Let our money become an opportunity for love.

**Congregation 2:** By the Spirit equip us for our ministry, mind and purse, muscle and spirit.

Reader: Which now of these three, thinkest thou, was neighbor unto him that fell among thieves? And he said, "He that showed mercy on him," Then said Jesus unto him, "Go, and do thou likewise."

Leader: Let us call our neighbors by name:

**Congregation 1:** Old folk, lonely and broken.

**Congregation 2:** Juvenile delinquent, outsider, unemployed.

**Congregation 1:** That one of another race, the homeless, the poor.

**Congregation 2:** The one next door ... beside me ...

**Congregation 1:** The neighbor in my own house.

**Congregation 1 and 2:** Even my enemy ...

Leader: Pure religion and undefiled is this visit to the fatherless and the widows in their affliction, and to keep oneself unspotted from the world.

Reader: O Christ, who called me a neighbor, and died that I might be a neighbor, give me grace to be a neighbor.

**Congregations 1 and 2:** Let us go and show mercy in the name of the Father and of the Son and of the Holy Spirit.

**The Offering**

**Hymn:** "They Cast Their Nets In Galilee"

**The Kyrie**

**The Lord's Prayer**
    Our Father in heaven:
        Holy be your name,
        Your kingdom come.
        Your will be done
            on earth as in heaven.
        Give us today our daily bread.
        Forgive us our sins,
            as we forgive those who sin against us.
        Save us in the time of trial,
            and deliver us from evil.
        For yours is the kingdom, the power,
            and glory forever. Amen.

**The Nicene Creed**

**Pastor:** In response to the holy Word proclaimed, let us pray for ourselves, that we may be faithful, and for all men, that they may find in the Church the one hope of God's call:

For the Church, built up with living stones into a temple for God in the Spirit.

For our pastors and for their ministry of praise and sanctification. (The prayer follows)

**The Benediction**

## A Service Based On Theological Concepts

(It is suggested that the readings be included in the material given to the congregation — except for staging directions, of course. In this way, the information will be available for future reference, and it will also make it easier for the cast, who read their parts.)

**Pastor:** O Lord, open my lips.

**Cong.:** **And my mouth shall speak your praise.**

**Pastor:** Be pleased, O God, to deliver me.

**Cong.:** **O Lord, make haste to help me.**

**All:** **Glory be to the Father and to the Son and to the Holy Spirit; as it was in the beginning, is now, and shall be forever and ever. Amen. Praise be to you.**

**The Psalm:** Psalm 25

**The Gloria Patri** (may be said or sung)

**The Lesson**

**The Kyrie** (may be said or sung)

**The Hymn:** "My Hope Is Built On Nothing Less"

**Meditation** (Readings on Theological Terms)

Pastor: We're all used to using and hearing words like "sin" and "forgiveness" and "justification," but do we really know what they mean? Maybe you're like most people, and use these words without really being aware of their full meaning. So, tonight, we want to spend some time in our meditation period in talking about these words and maybe explaining them a bit. I've asked some of our friends to help me with these words, and we hope that you'll go home tonight with a better idea of what much of our faith means. First of all, _____ will tell us about the meaning of the word "sin."

1st Boy: The most frequently used word for "sin" in the New Testament is a word that literally means "the departure from the way of righteousness." Let me show you what this means *(holds up a large picture of a road marked "righteousness" or "right living," with another road running parallel to it, marked "sin." Or, if you prefer, the picture can be that of a target marked "right living" and the arrow marked "sin" is then alongside it rather than in the target).* You see from the picture that sin means going the wrong way (or missing the target). But it's more than just missing the way — it's doing it deliberately and going away from God. You know, God has given man freedom of choice when it comes to accepting or rejecting him. And sin can be seen as the result of man's using this freedom to find his security in some human thing, such as money or power or sex, rather than relying totally on God. So, sin is really rebellion against God. But how does this fit into our Lenten study? Well, sin is action which is opposed to God's divine laws, and the act of sinning brings about guilt and separation from God. But Jesus, by his death and resurrection, has become the victor over sin. So, finally, we come to the definition of sin which is given us in John 16:9 — sin is lack of faith in Jesus. And that's simple enough to understand. So, let's go back to our picture — true faith in Jesus and reliance on him means that the road comes back and joins the road that leads to righteousness (or the arrow that reaches the target). Now, of course, just having faith in Jesus isn't going to keep us from sinning, but it will

|           | show us the way that we should follow. And we are helped by grace. _____, will you tell us about the meaning of grace? |
|-----------|---|
| 1st Girl: | Well, all right. But I can't show you a picture to explain grace. All I can do is ask you to use your imaginations. Picture to yourself a huge gift box — big enough to take in the whole world. Because that's what grace is — a gift from God to the world. You know, all our lives we've been getting gifts that we didn't deserve. I'm sure we can all remember times when we were little that we were anything but loving, obedient children. But that didn't keep us from getting presents on our birthdays and at Christmas. And we certainly can't claim to be any better now. But still we aren't denied gifts from our friends and from the people who love us. Because they understand that sometimes we behave badly, but still they love us. And that's the way it is with God. We kick over the traces all the time, but he doesn't stop loving us. You remember the stories in the Old Testament of all the times that the Israelites disobeyed God and broke faith with him. But did God say, "All right. Two can play at that game. You break faith with me — I'll break faith with you!" No, of course not. No matter how often the people were faithless, God still remained faithful to them. And that's really what grace is — God's ultimate faithfulness to his chosen people. For Saint Paul, this was shown in the Incarnation and the Atonement, the acts by which God in Christ showed his favor to men. And how does Paul say that we earn this grace? Well, as a matter of fact, we can't. There's no way that we can pile up credits toward so many ounces or pounds of grace. And, what's more, we don't have to. We have all the grace we'll ever need. And it's free! We certainly don't deserve it, but, even so, God gives it to us freely, just because he loves us so much. And he doesn't give it |

just to Lutherans or Methodists or Catholics. Not just to Americans or British or Africans. No, it is available for all the people of the world. All we have to do is accept it in faith. It's a wonderful word to remember. In fact, it's such a wonderful word that it's almost a one-word summary of the entire biblical message. But there's another word that goes along with this which we often find hard to understand — the word "justification." _____, will you explain this word to us?

2nd Boy: Yes, I'd like to do that. I'd like for you to take a look at this coin that I have with me. *(Holds up a large drawing of a coin.)* On this we have printed the word PENITENCE and on the other side *(turns it around)* we have the word FAITH. And these two words are the important ones if we are to understand justification. You know, a lot of people are hung up on the idea of a law court and justice when this word comes up. And, in a sense, they're right. But that idea doesn't carry us far enough. It's true enough that God plays the part of the judge, but divine justification means much more than just the idea of punishment of sin. It even means more than a guilty man being acquitted. Actually, it means the activity of God in which he restores man to goodness and the right relationship with himself. And I want you to pay attention to that word — activity — not mine, but God's! I can't begin to justify myself, only God can do it for me. And that he does through the gift of grace that _____ told us about. And, as _____ said, we need faith in Christ and his atoning work. So that sort of ties our first two words in with this one, doesn't it? Well, of course, I think you'll find that this is true of all our words. Because the Christ event is an interwoven event, which touches on our lives at all points. But how about the other side of our coin? We've talked about the FAITH side, but how about the PENITENCE side? Well, of course, that's a little easier to understand in the idea of a judge and justice. If I have broken a law, and I'm sorry that I did so, and want to make amends, the judge might possibly say, "Well, in view of your penitent attitude, I suspend judgment." And God says that, too. "Because you are sorry that you have broken my law, and because Jesus has already paid the penalty for you, I release you from judgment, and restore you to my favor." So, you see, justification isn't really hard to understand — it's just another way of saying that God accepts us to himself because of his grace and the atoning death of Jesus on the cross. Now, there's another word that has been used a few times, and that should be explained. _____, will you tell us about atonement?

2nd Girl: Well, I'm afraid that in a lot of ways I'm going to be repeating what the others have already said. But maybe I can carry their thoughts one step further. The word "atonement" itself doesn't occur in the New Testament; in fact, the English word "atone" comes from the phrase "at one," which explains it fairly well. The atonement is God's means of making men "at one" with him again, and it's related entirely to Jesus Christ and his coming to earth and, especially, to his death on the cross. But, since we are human and don't have divine understanding, we are always looking for words which will describe the things which we can't understand. And so three words, in particular, were used to describe the Atonement. First of all, there was the word which indicated a ransom. This was a familiar idea to the people of the New Testament times because it was the same word which was used when slaves paid a certain amount to win their release. *(Hold up a scroll.)* This is a scroll of manumission, which was proof for the slave that he had bought his freedom There is also the word "redemption," which means buying back a slave or captive, making him free by the payment, again, of a ransom, and there is the simple word "bought." This also implies the payment of a price, and it belongs to the same context of thought as the payment of a ransom. All of these made it easy to consider the Atonement in such a way that the life of Christ was actually an agreed price paid to secure men freedom from bondage to Satan, although the men who formulated this idea never made it clear to whom this ransom is to be paid. Really, it is not possible for men to understand **how** Christ has done his atoning work; it is only necessary that we know and believe that he has done so. There was a wall of estrangement between God and humankind and Jesus has broken down that wall and reconciled man and God. And that's the topic for our next speaker. _____, will you tell us about reconciliation?

3rd Boy: Well, the word reconciliation means the restoration of people to fellowship with God. Now it's important that we put it that way — it's the reconciliation of people to God, not of God to people. God hasn't drawn away from us, but we have drawn away from him, and have built the walls between us that keep us from enjoying communion with him. But because of Christ's sacrificial death, these walls have been destroyed, and we can again consider ourselves in God's favor. Maybe you will be able to better understand everything we have been saying if you will follow with us through the responsive liturgy!

Leader: What creates walls between people and nations?

**Congregation 1:** Fear! For many reasons we fear one another, and to fear people is to be separated from them.

**Congregation 2:** Pride! When we are confronted by the truth about ourselves, our pride keeps us from facing our inadequacies. We are separated from others who might free us and allow us to know them.

**Congregation 1:** Power! Wanting control lives and governments we build walls of concrete or wood or ideas, and lock ourselves in as well as lock others out.

**Congregation 2:** Hate! We are unable or unwilling to love each other. We hate people we do not know, and we wish them dead. Death of recognition is a hard, cold wall.

Leader: Can these walls be broken down?

All: Indeed! But we like the walls. They make us secure. As long as no one scales the walls there is a kind of peace, or should we say silence — the silence of the dead. We seem to prefer the peace of death to the struggles of life.

Leader: But can these walls be broken down?

**Congregation 1:** Yes, with faith. If we dare to trust one another, if we dare to trust the Giver of all life, then fear can be banished and so, too, the wall made of it. But both sides of the wall must trust each other, and trust must have a foundation on which to build understanding.

**Congregation 2:** Humility breaks walls of pride. Then we who dare to see ourselves as we are can begin to build relationships out of what is really there. But humility must first be cultivated in ourselves.

**Congregation 1:** Love is the perfect breaker of walls that separate people. We all need the confirmation of love. Others need such love from us. We all need to know that God cares for us.

Leader: If what you say is true, the walls come down only at tremendous cost to us as we try to break them down.

All: Sometimes the cost is death. Jesus died on a cross but, though he was killed, he loved the killers. The walls of hate and power and pride and fear could not prevail.

Leader: "For he is our peace, who has made us both one, and has broken down the dividing wall of hostility" (Ephesians 2:14).

All: Help us, Father, where we are, begin to tear down the walls of our own isolation from people — our little fears of change, our personal prejudices, our protective natures. Show us how wonderful a view we get of people when the walls come down.

3rd Boy: And now there's one final word that we want to consider — the word "church." _____, will you tell us about the church?

3rd Girl: Yes, of course, I will. I have here a picture here of church *(holds up a large picture of a church)*, and that is exactly what it is — a church. By that I mean that it is a building, which we call a church, in which people gather to worship. But what we are interested in especially is the Church, and there's a big difference. The Church is composed of all the people all over the world who share the same faith in Jesus Christ as their Lord and who acknowledge his saving grace in their lives. There are denominational churches — we speak of the

Lutheran Church, the Episcopalian Church, the Catholic Church, and such, but these are just labels. The important thing that we have to remember is that the Church is composed of all those who believe. One of the fundamental principles of Protestantism is the priesthood of all believers. This means that we all have access to God — that is, that we can pray to him directly, and we don't have to go through mediators; that we each face God in our own right, that is, no one can live our faith for us; and we are each called to be priests in the sense that we should tell others about Christ and our faith. In this way, the Church is built of living relationships between persons, showing the Spirit of Jesus Christ, and it is the instrument of God's continuing work in the world. And our obligation is to make this Church known to all people. Well, that's our explanation of some of the words which we use all the time and maybe don't always understand. And now we'd like to conclude our service tonight with the following liturgy:

Pastor: Thank God, the God and Father of our Lord Jesus Christ, that in his great mercy we have been born again into a life of hope, through Christ's rising from the dead!

All: Amen.

Pastor: Why did God create us?

All: To praise him forever.

Pastor: The proof of God's amazing love is this: that it was while we were sinners Christ died for us. It is in the same Jesus, because we have faith in him, that we dare with confidence to approach God. Let us admit our guilt before God.

All: Father, we have done wrong; by not caring when we should have loved; by our indifference to the cry of need; and by hating and ignoring our neighbors. We have rejected the way of your Son, and no longer deserve to be called your children. O God, we cannot help ourselves; forgive us; through Jesus Christ our Lord. Amen.

Pastor: This statement is completely reliable and should be universally accepted: Jesus Christ entered the world to rescue sinners. He personally bore our sins in his body on the cross, so that we might be dead to sin and be alive to all that is good.

All: Amen. You are the Lord, Giver of mercy! You are the Christ, Giver of mercy! You are the Lord, Giver of mercy!

Pastor: Let us pray.

O God, tell us what we need to hear and show us what we ought to do to obey your Son, Jesus Christ.

All: Amen.

Pastor: Let us say what we believe.

All: This is the good news which we received, in which we stand, and by which we are saved: that Christ died for sins according to the Scriptures, that he was buried, that he was raised on the third day; and that he appeared to Peter, then to the Twelve and to many faithful witnesses.

We believe he is the Christ, the Son of the Living God. He is the First and the Last, the Beginning and the End. He is our Lord and our God. Amen.

Pastor: The Lord is risen.

All: He is risen indeed.

Pastor: Lift up your hearts.

All: We lift them up to the Lord.

Pastor: Let us glorify God.

All: For all his goodness to us.

Pastor: O God our Father, creator of this pleasant world and giver of all good things, we thank you for our home on earth and for the joy of living. We praise you for your love in Jesus Christ, who came to set things right, who died rejected on the cross and rose triumphant from the dead; because he lives, we live to praise you, Father, Son, and Holy Spirit, our God forever.

All: O God, who called us from death to life: we give ourselves to you; and with the church through all ages, we thank you for your saving love in Jesus Christ our Lord. Amen.

Pastor: God of our fathers: we praise you for all your servants who, having been faithful to you on earth, now live with you in heaven. Keep us in fellowship with them until we meet with all your children in the joy of the kingdom; through Jesus Christ our Lord.

All: Our Father in heaven, may your name be honored. May your kingdom come and your will be done on earth as it is in heaven. Give us today the food we need; and forgive us our sins as we forgive those who have wronged us. Keep us clear of temptation, and save us from evil. For the kingdom and the power and glory are yours forever. Amen.

Pastor: And now go out into the world in peace; have courage; hold on to what is good; return no one evil for evil; strengthen the fainthearted; support the weak; help the suffering; honor all people; love and serve the Lord, rejoicing in the power of the Holy Spirit.

Living always in the grace of the Lord Jesus Christ and the love of God and the fellowship of the Holy Spirit.

The Lord watch between you and me, when we are absent one from the other. Amen.

## A Service Based On The Sacrament Of Baptism

**Pastor:** O Lord, open my lips.

**Cong.:** And my mouth shall speak your praise.

**Pastor:** Be pleased, O God, to deliver me.

**Cong.:** O Lord, make haste to help me.

**All:** Glory be to the Father and to the Son and to the Holy Spirit; as it was in the beginning, is now, and shall be forever and ever. Amen. Praise be to you.

**The Psalm:** Psalm 23

**The Gloria Patri** (may be said or sung)

**The Lesson**

**The Kyrie**
Jesus, Lamb of God:
 have mercy on us.
Jesus, bearer of our sins:
 have mercy on us.
Jesus, redeemer of the world:
 give us your peace.

**The Hymn:** "Breathe On Me, Breath Of God"

**Meditation** (Based on the Sacrament of Baptism)

(Requires two boys and two girls in dialogue with the pastor.)

1st Girl: I went to a baptism with a friend of mine the other day, and do you know what? They had to go down the river, and everybody who was being baptized had to put on special clothes and go into the water. Boy!

2nd Girl: So, what's wrong with that? Seems to me it's better than just dropping a little water on a baby's head and saying, "There now, you're all washed clean." That doesn't make sense. How can a few little drops of water make anybody clean?

1st Boy: What would you like, a compromise? Maybe they could take the baby and duck his head into the water. How would you like that?

2nd Boy: That's not funny, _____. We know from our catechisms why we baptize the way that we do. But I really don't understand why we're talking about baptism now. I thought we were going to use these evenings to talk about things connected with Lent.

Pastor: Yes, we are. Don't you think baptism has anything to do with Lent? Let me remind you of the words that Saint Paul wrote to the Romans: "Have you forgotten that when we were baptized into union with Christ Jesus we were baptized into his death? By baptism we were buried with him, and lay dead, in order that, as Christ was raised from the dead in the splendor of the Father, so also we might set our feet upon the new path of life." Now that might be a little hard to understand. But, after all, Lent is connected with death, and, finally, resurrection. So it seems appropriate to talk about baptism tonight. You know, it often bothers me that so many people will very conscientiously bring their children to be baptized, and will themselves go to Communion regularly, but they don't really think about what they're doing when they engage in these acts. So maybe tonight we can have a sort of refresher course. What do you think?

2nd Boy: I think that's a good idea. After all, we're Christians and Jesus started the whole baptism idea, so I think we should know all we can about it.

1st Girl: Well, I guess you'd better start learning right now, _____. Jesus didn't "start the whole baptism idea." It was an old custom by the time he was born. I don't remember where I read that, but I'm sure I did, because I used to think the same that you did. Pastor, is it really true that baptism is much older than Christianity?

Pastor: Yes, in one sense this is certainly true. All known religions have some method worked into them by which a person can be "washed clean" from his sins. And, of course, this is what baptism is — a washing clean. Our word comes from a Greek word, *baptidzo*, which means to wash, or to dip. And I suppose that would imply that _____'s friend's church is using the proper method, by going to the river and dipping in. But we don't think that's really necessary. But we'll talk about that in a minute. Right now I'd like to clear up this idea that Jesus started baptism. I can think of one very good reason why that can't be so. Can any one else think of why?

2nd Girl: I can. Because Jesus himself was baptized by John the Baptist. But who baptized John then?

1st Boy: I think I know the answer to that. I read that he was probably a member of the community at Qumran. And the excavations there show that they went in for the baptism in a big way. Isn't that right, pastor?

Pastor: Well, I can't say for sure that John was an Essene, as the people who lived in Qumran were called. I do know that many scholars believe that he was, and the evidence would certainly seem to point that way. But we don't know that much about him. And anyway, it isn't really important where he came from. The Bible tells us all that we need to know about him — that he was the one who told the world that Jesus was coming, and that he then started Jesus on his ministry when he baptized him.

1st Boy: What do you mean, started him on his ministry?

Pastor: Well, if you'll read Matthew, you'll find that Jesus was baptized, then he went into the wilderness where he was tempted by the Devil, and then he started his public life. So we can see that this baptism was a public announcement, just as our baptism is a public announcement that we are Christians.

2nd Boy: Did all the other religions baptize with water, too?

Pastor: No, there were all sorts of ways. Some of them, such as "baptizing with fire" are still in use today. The ancient Persians had a particularly messy way. The candidate for baptism had to stand in a pit, and a bull was slaughtered above him, so that the blood of the bull ran down over him. This was to wash away his sins in the blood of the bull and give the candidate strength. There were other even worse methods. But the important thing to remember is that the basic idea is the same in all methods — the washing away of sins and impurities, so that the new person who emerges is clean — spiritually, that is.

1st Girl: You said that we'd talk about why we don't have to be dipped. Will you do that now?

Pastor: Yes, but I think you already know the answer to that. At least, I hope you do. You remember that in our catechism classes we talked about how baptism works. Remember? And what did Luther say in his catechism that is the basic ingredient in baptism that makes the water effective?

1st Girl:     I know. It's faith that the water is going to work. It's not just the water. And we get the faith from hearing the Word from our preachers and teachers.

Pastor:     Yes, that's right. We could use anything, if we didn't have water handy. But there are very few places where we can't have access to water, so it's sort of a universal symbol. But whatever we use, it won't work unless we believe that it will. It's the faith that baptizes, not the water at all. And when the faith is there, the desire to make ourselves as clean as possible is there, too. We don't go visiting our closest friends without making ourselves presentable, do we? And, in the same way, we don't visit God without making ourselves spiritually presentable. And that's really what baptism is. Spiritual cleansing.

2nd Girl:     Well, I still don't understand. If I take a shower in the morning, I'm clean, sure. But I'm not going to stay clean all day. I have to take a bath again the next morning. Or even another one during the day, if I'm going out. So why don't I have to be baptized every day? How can I stay clean spiritually? On the one hand, the Church tells me that I've been made clean, and on the other hand, it tells me that I sin all the time. Doesn't make sense.

Pastor:     Well, I think you have the same idea that a lot of people have — that baptism is some kind of magic wand that will automatically keep you from sinning again. And of course that's not true at all. Baptism makes you a child of God — that is, by the act of baptism you declare yourself to be a Christian, but you are still a human being, and so you still sin all the time. So we can't just rest on our laurels and say, "Well, now I'm baptized, so I can't really sin very badly. And if I do, God will forgive me." It's just not that simple. Actually, every day we have to renew our baptismal vows. It's not enough to be baptized once and let it go at that. We have to work at being Christians, you know. And that work involves constant awareness that we are always breaking God's commandments, and constant repentance for that sinning. Do you understand that?

2nd Girl: Well, yes. I guess I understand that all right. But what about babies? You baptize them when they're just a few weeks old, and they certainly don't sin. Or if they did, they wouldn't know about it.

1st Boy: I know about that. That's why we have sponsors. They take the place of the baby's conscience, sort of, until he's old enough to know for himself that he's a sinner. That's why we go to confirmation classes, so that we can learn all these things.

Pastor: That's right. You know, there was a time when people waited to be baptized until they were dying. They thought the same way, that you did, _____.
They figured that if baptism was going to take away their sins, they'd get in all the sinning they could, and then repent and be baptized when they were on their deathbeds and not in much danger of sinning any more. Well, of course, that's just reading the whole thing wrong. That's like making a bargain with God — "You close your eyes, God, to what I'm doing, and when I get ready to die, then I'll let you get your licks in." But, of course, we can't make deals with God. We either accept him and his laws, and try to live our lives the way that he wants us to, or we say, "Forget it. I'm going to do things my way. And my way doesn't include you and your rules, God!"

2nd Boy: Well, I think we can all see that, all right. And I think that I can see now how we can tie baptism in with our

|           | Lenten studies. Jesus did everything that we have to do to make ourselves acceptable to God, and that included being baptized. That was part of Jesus' human nature, that he had to do everything that we're expected to do. And that means that we have to follow his guidelines, and do things like he did. And I guess that means that maybe we'll have to suffer some before we die, and that we'll all have to die sometime. But because we know the story of Lent, and especially the story of Easter, we don't have to be afraid. Because we were baptized, we are children of God, and that makes Jesus our brother. And because he died and then rose again, that means that we can be sure that we will rise again, too. Is that the real way that baptism is tied up with Lent? |
|-----------|---|
| Pastor:   | Yes, _____, I think you've really made it clear. Jesus is our brother, and through baptism we became a member of his family, and have been accepted by his Father and ours. I think that maybe we all understand our Christian heritage a little better now, don't we? And maybe to make it a little more specific, next week we can talk about the Lord's Supper. Would you like that? All right. We'll do that. And now let's sing about the sacrament of baptism. |

**Hymn:** "Love Divine, All Loves Excelling"

**The Creed**

**The Lord's Prayer**

A soloist may sing the Thank The Lord and The Perpetual Petitions. Otherwise, they can be said, but they are more effective if sung.

**The Benediction**

## A Service Based On The Sacrament Of The Altar

**Pastor:** O Lord, open my lips.

**Cong.:** **And my mouth shall speak your praise.**

**Pastor:** Be pleased, O God, to deliver me.

**Cong.:** **O Lord, make haste to help me.**

**All:** **Glory be to the Father and to the Son and to the Holy Spirit; as it was in the beginning, is now, and shall be forever and ever. Amen. Praise be to you.**

**The Psalm:** Psalm 40

**The Gloria Patri** (may be said or sung)

**The Lesson**

**The Kyrie**
    Jesus, Lamb of God:
      have mercy on us.
    Jesus, bearer of our sins:
      have mercy on us.
    Jesus, redeemer of the world:
      give us your peace.

**The Hymn:** "Break Now The Bread Of Life"

**Meditation** (Based on the Sacrament of the Altar)

(Requires two boys and two girls in dialogue with the pastor.)

Pastor: You remember that last week we decided that this week we'd talk about the Lord's Supper? Well, have any of you been doing any thinking about it this week?

1st Boy: Yes, I have, and I have a question. You said last week that baptism is much older than Christianity. Is the same thing true for the Lord's Supper?

Pastor: Well, before I give you an answer, why don't we see if someone else has an idea on this?

1st Girl: Well, for one thing, it can't very well be the **Lord's** Supper unless it's about Jesus, can it? I mean, after all, he is the Lord, so it must be about him. Right?

Pastor: Well, right and wrong. It is about our Lord, Jesus Christ, so in that you're right. But there were a lot of things said about him long before he was ever born, so that means that you could be wrong, too. Anyone else have an idea?

2nd Girl: Yes, I know where the idea comes from. I know that the Gospel says that Jesus wanted to spend the Passover with his disciples, and that it was during the Passover meal that he instituted the Lord's Supper. And the Passover is really old. It goes way back to the Exodus.

Pastor: That's fine, _____. You've really done your homework. Yes, it's true that the Lord's Supper as we know it grew out of the Passover celebrations. Let me tell you about the Passover. The Passover is a very solemn time for Jews. In fact, it is the most solemn and sacred time in their year. It is celebrated every year in commemoration of the events recorded in the book of Exodus. The people of Israel were being held as slaves in the land of Egypt, and God had sent Moses to the Pharaoh to order him to release the Israelites. However, Pharaoh refused, and God, through Moses, sent ten plagues on the land. They were designed to soften the Pharaoh's heart, so that he could be persuaded to let the people go away from Egypt.

The first plague was the turning of the Nile from water into blood; this didn't work, so God sent a second plague, which was an invasion of frogs into the land; that didn't work either, and so next came lice, and then flies, and then the cattle all died. And still it wasn't enough to soften up the Pharaoh, and so God sent a plague of boils, and then hail, which was a very rare occurrence in the land of Egypt. Still nothing. So again God sent a plague, this time of locusts, which devastated the land. Then God refused to let the sun rise, so that there was darkness over the whole land for three days. And still the Pharaoh was stubborn, and wouldn't let the people go. And so, finally, God said that the firstborn male, both man and animal, would have to die.

However, God didn't want to destroy his own people in the process, and so he told Moses, "Tell your people to kill a lamb, one year old, a male, without any spots or blemishes on it. Put some of the blood from this lamb on your two doorposts, and this will be a sign." He said that wherever he saw this blood he would pass over the house and the plague wouldn't strike in that house. And he said that they should roast the lamb and eat it. And God said, "And this shall be unto you a memorial, and you will keep it a feast unto the Lord throughout all generations. And it shall come to pass, when your children shall say unto you, 'What mean ye by this service?' that ye shall answer, 'It is the sacrifice of the Lord's Passover, who passed over the houses of the children of Israel in Egypt, when he slew the Egyptians and spared us.' "

What's more, Moses gave the people specific instrucions. As they ate this meal, the people were supposed to be ready for instant flight. Apparently they had to eat standing up, because Moses said, "In this manner shall ye eat it, with your staff in your hand, and you shall eat it in haste." So, of course, the Israelites did what Moses told them, and at midnight the Lord killed all the firstborn in the land, including the oldest son of the Pharaoh. And that was the turning point. When Pharaoh found that his son was dead, he called Moses and said, "Rise up, go forth, both you and the people of Israel, to serve your Lord. Take your people, your flocks, and be gone."

But there was little time then to bake bread, so they set out with their kneading troughs on their heads, and then, later, when they were hungry, they stopped and baked the bread. But the women hadn't had time to let it rise, so it was flat and hard. And then, as time went on, and the people were settled in a land of their own, every year they baked this hard, flat bread as a symbol in memory of the "Bread of Affliction" that they ate on their journey away from Egypt. And, so that the people would never forget what he had done for them, God told them that every year they should celebrate the Feast of the Passover. If any of you have any Jewish friends, you'll know that they still celebrate this festival today in exactly the same way that they did over 3,000 years ago! And, of course, it was celebrated in that way when Jesus was alive.

And, as _____ said, it was at the Passover that Jesus instituted the Lord's Supper. You see, he knew that in just a few days he was going to die. And, of course, he also knew that all of the events that were going to happen were going to be terribly confusing to his disciples. And he knew that they would wonder about a lot of things. So he tried to make it as easy for them as he could. And, although they were all Jews — Jesus, too, remember — he had come to do away with many of the Old Testament rules, and he wanted them to know this. Of course, at the Passover, there was constant sacrificing going on in the Temple, because this was one of the things that God had said a long time before that he demanded from the people. So Jesus was able to use the symbolism of the sacrifice to tell them about what his death was going to accomplish.

He took a piece of bread and prayed over it and then passed out pieces to his disciples, and said to them, "Take this and eat it; this is my Body, which is given for you." That, of course, would refer to the body of the sacrificial animal which is laid on the altar and killed as an offering to God. Then he took the wine and said, "All of you drink of this. It is the blood of the New Covenant which is poured out for you and for many for the forgiveness of sins." By the New Covenant he meant that the Old Testament covenant between God and man was no longer necessary, because Jesus was bringing a new order into the world. And, of course, the blood, again, refers to the sacrifices. And he said that we should do this constantly, having faith that he is with us when we commune, and that he will keep his promises. And, you know, the wonderful thing about it is that this communion is so personal. In the Communion service, Jesus bends down and gives his love directly to me. It's a wonderful thing.

2nd Boy: Yes. I guess we all know most of that. But there's something that I've never really been able to understand. I know that when I go to Communion I get a wafer because it doesn't taste like anything else, and I get wine because it tastes like wine. But we're taught, and you just said, that we're really getting the body and blood of Christ. I can't understand that. Can you explain it to me?

Pastor: Well, since I'm only human, I can't really understand it, either. Just as I can't understand how Jesus can be here with us and with someone in Africa and with someone else in Alaska, all at the same time. These things are mysteries that the human mind just can't imagine, but because Jesus says that they are so, then we accept them on faith and believe them. And in the same way, because Jesus said that the bread was his Body, and the wine was his Blood, then we believe that this is so.

1st Girl: Ugh, that always sounds to me as if I was eating a human being. It's like being a cannibal.

Pastor: Well, perhaps in a way that's true. Oh, don't looked so shocked. I'm not being blasphemous. But remember last week we talked about the different religions that there have been in the world, and the ways in which they are alike. Well, another one of the ways in which they're alike is that ancient people believed that, by eating a bit of flesh or drinking some of the blood of a dead hero, they could get some of his courage and strength. Of course, by the time that Jesus lived, people were a little more sophisticated, but even so, the idea was still there that they could become a part of divinity by eating and drinking with him. And this is what Jesus is saying. "By eating the wafer and drinking the wine — WITH FAITH THAT I AM PRESENT IN THEM IN SOME WAY — you become a part of Me." Does that seem at all reasonable to you? It's not magic, or anything like that. It's the same thing that we said last week — if I have faith that the water of baptism will clean me and rid me of my sins, then it will do so. And the same thing is true of the Lord's Supper. If I have faith that Jesus is present in the bread and the wine, they will have the power to release me from my sins, and make me able to serve my Lord as he wants me to.

1st Boy: I have a friend who goes to a different church, and he says that it's wrong to drink wine at Communion. In his church they serve grape juice. What about that? Who's right?

1st Girl: Oh, I know the answer to that. I had a friend who belonged to a church like that. And she told me that her church doesn't believe in smoking or drinking anything with alcohol in it and that sort of thing. So, since wine has alcohol, they have to drink grape juice instead. I guess it's the same way that we accept the whole idea of Communion. We can't say if they're right or we're right. If we both believe that Jesus is present in whatever we're drinking, and we are sure that he can forgive us our sins, it doesn't really matter what means we use. Is that right, pastor?

Pastor: You're not only right about that, _____, but I'm very happy to hear you say it. You're showing true Christian charity by accepting the right of other people to worship in their own way. Of course, I want you to accept the way our church does things, but I also want you to know that other people are as devoted to their churches and their ways of worshiping as we are. If everyone could accept the other person in that way, the world would be a lot better off. Don't you agree? Do you remember that last week we sang a special song about baptism? Well, tonight we have one that the same man wrote about the Lord's Supper. Let's sing it, shall we?

**Hymn:** "O Word Of God Incarnate"

**The Creed**

**The Lord's Prayer**

A soloist may sing the Thank You Lord and The Perpetual Petitions. Otherwise, they can be said, but they are more effective if sung.

**The Benediction**

www.ingramcontent.com/pod-product-compliance
Lightning Source LLC
Chambersburg PA
CBHW071800040426
42446CB00012B/2645